RABBITS

Keith Lawrence BVSc, MRCVS

HAMLYN

Introduction

All of the pet breeds of rabbits are derived from the wild rabbit. The rabbit was introduced into Britain after the Norman Conquest in the eleventh century, and whilst it is unlikely that it was kept as a pet, its value as a food was certainly recognized. Throughout the Middle Ages, artificial mounds or warrens were constructed to ensure this source of winter food. Rabbits were first tamed and selectively bred in the monasteries and have been kept as pets since the nineteenth century, being taken to Australia where they escaped and became a serious pest. From these small beginnings have developed more than 60 fancy breeds.

Rabbits are a popular pet, being responsive and very

Wild rabbits are very gregarious and live together in large complex burrows.

easily tamed. They are ideal pets for the older child who can take on the responsibility for their daily needs. Most rabbits are good natured and will tolerate mis-handling by young children. It is important to choose a size of rabbit which the child can manage. Dwarf rabbits weigh about 1kg (2lb) and can be handled with ease by a young child, but a Flemish Giant weighing 7-10kg (15-22lb) requires an adult to help with the handling. Most crossbred pet shop rabbits weigh about 2-3kg (4-7lb). Rabbits can live for up to 12 years but this is unusual and many rabbits show signs of senility from 5-6 years of age. Many of the longer-lived individuals tend to be unmated female rabbits.

Choosing and buying a rabbit

There are more than 60 recognized breeds of rabbits, and often more than 20 colour variations within a breed. Pure-bred rabbits are divided into 'fancy breeds' and 'fur breeds'. Many pet shop rabbits are crossbreds, but without seeing the parents, it will often be difficult to know how large they will grow. Rabbits can be safely kept with guinea pigs and tortoises.

Rabbits can be bought from a number of sources: a friend whose rabbit has had a litter, a breeder who specializes in one particular breed of rabbit or a pet shop. It should be 6-8 weeks old. Always examine the rabbit thoroughly before purchase. Look at the rabbits in the pen before handling them. They should move about

Adult rabbits come in all sizes: a New Zealand White is much bigger than a Chincilla Netherland Dwarf.

freely and the breathing should be regular and unforced, with usually about 40-60 breaths per minute. Even when at rest the ears are usually pricked and the animals are watchful. Droppings in the pen are usually dry and well-formed and brown in colour. Pick the rabbit up and assess its condition. If you can feel the spine and ribs easily the rabbit is thin and should not be purchased. If the animal is of a reasonable size, check the points in the following table.

Signs of health

Head

Nose Free from discharge, no scabs. In a healthy rabbit it will be seen to be twitching rhythmically.

Eyes Clean and bright, not watery, no mattery discharge or puffiness around the eye.

Teeth Clean, not overlong and growing parallel.

Ears Clean, no waxy discharge or encrustations.

Body

Skin Clean, free from scurf and cyst-like swellings, supple with no areas of reddenning or itchiness.

Coat Clean, sleek and shining. Look for parasites and bare patches.

Limbs Claws evenly worn and short. Look on the inside of each forelimb at wrist level, check to see if it is damp and discoloured. A rabbit with a cold will wipe its nose on this area of the foreleg known as the 'rabbit's handkerchief'. Hindlegs should be checked for sores and swellings.

Anus The anus should be clean and unstained. Staining usually means diarrhoea.

Breeds

Large Breeds

Belgian Hare It resembles a hare both in shape and size, but it is a rabbit and makes a good pet. It is chestnut in colour with bold hazel eyes. Weight 3·5-4kg (7-9lb).

Beveren There are four colorations available, the oldest of which is the blue which originated in the 1890s. They have a dense, silky and lustrous coat. Weight 3·5-4·5kg (7-10lb).

If you buy a rabbit from a pet shop, it will probably be a crossbred like this one. They can give as much enjoyment as pure-bred rabbits.

British Giant The largest of the British rabbits. There are many different coat and eye colours. Weight 5·5-7kg (12-15lb).

Californian Although this rabbit is bred mainly for meat, it is very docile and makes a good pet. The coat is white with black or chocolate coloured patches on the nose, ears, feet and tail. The markings are similar to those of a Siamese cat. Weight 3·5-5kg (7-11lb).

Flemish Giant This is the largest of the domestic breeds, being principally bred for meat. This rabbit needs a very large hutch. It has steel grey fur flecked with black. Weight 5·5-10kg (12-22lb).

Lop The lop-eared rabbit is the oldest of the fancy breeds, the ears measuring up to 70cm (28in). The ears appear normal until the rabbit is about 14 days old when they begin to droop. A full range of colours have been bred. There are three main types of lop-eared rabbit: the English Lop, weight 6·5-9kg (14-20lb); the French Lop, weight 4·5-5·5kg (9-12lb); the Dwarf Lop, weight 2kg (4½lb).

New Zealand White Usually bred for meat or the fur trade, but being docile they are quite suitable pets. They have a dense white coat and pink eyes. Weight 4-5kg (9-11lb).

Medium-sized Breeds

Angora This is a wool producing rabbit. The coat needs a lot of attention, and so it is not a beginner's rabbit. There are several colours. Weight 2·5-2·7kg (5½-6lb).

Chinchilla This rabbit was originally bred for the fur, which is soft and fine. It is deep slate in colour overlaid with bands of pearl white and tipped with black. It is a

very attractive rabbit and makes an excellent pet.
Dutch This very popular show breed also make excellent
pets. The coat is smooth and shiny, lying close to the

(Top to bottom) A Belgian Hare, an English rabbit, an English
lop-eared rabbit and a Dutch rabbit.

body. The basic colour is white combined with one other colour, blue and grey being the most popular. There is usually a white blaze and shoulder with a coloured abdomen, ears, cheeks and eyes. Weight 2-2·5kg (4½-5½lb).

English This popular breed is white with a coloured nose, ears and eyes and with chains of spots on the flanks. Weight 2·5-3·5kg (5½-8lb).

Harlequin A long-eared rabbit with attractive and unusual markings reminiscent of a chess board. Black and orange are the most popular colours. The black and white variety is called a Magpie. Weight 2·7-3·6kg (7-8lb).

Rex This is a collective name for a whole range of rabbits that differ in colour patterns and eye colour. The common factor is their coat which is like velvet and has no long guard hairs. Weight 2·5-3·6kg (5½-8lb).

Small Breeds

Himalayan This is a very attractive patterned rabbit with the same colour points as the Siamese cat. The main colour is white with the nose, ears, tail and feet coloured black, blue, lilac or chocolate. The young are all white until they leave the nest when the colours start to appear. Weight 2-2·5kg (4½-5½lb).

Netherland Dwarf This breed undoubtedly makes the best pet for the small child. These delightful rabbits when fully grown will sit in the palm of the hand. Two points to look for are small ears, less than 5cm (2in), and large bright eyes. There are many different colours. Weight 0·9kg (2lb).

Polish Although about the same size as the Netherland Dwarf, they are more hare-like, with longer ears and limbs. Weight 1kg (2¼lb).

Housing

Rabbits are traditionally housed in hutches. A well-built, roomy, draught-proof and dry hutch is basic to a rabbit's welfare. The hutch design will differ slightly depending on whether the rabbit is to be kept indoors or outside. The basic hutch is a cage sub-divided into two interconnecting sections. One section is fitted with a wire mesh door of 2cm (¾in) chicken wire, the other is fitted with a solidly built wooden door to enable the rabbit to shelter from the elements, and to sleep undisturbed at night.

The hutch must be raised a minimum of 23cm (9in) from the ground to allow a free circulation of air around the cage, and to give protection from rising damp, frost and predators. Raising the hutch to table top height will make cleaning and feeding much easier. If the rabbit is housed in a garage, it should not have to share it with the family car, because rabbits are very susceptible to exhaust fumes. In any case, the shed or garage must be well ventilated.

If the hutch is located outside, it must have a sloping roof to throw off the rain. A minimum height difference of 2½cm (1in) between the front and back of the roof will produce a suitable pitch. If the roof projects 12-15cm (5-6in) beyond the front of the hutch it will give added protection. The roof should be covered in roofing felt to make it waterproof.

The size of the hutch depends on the size of the rabbit. For a single medium sized rabbit, a hutch 120cm x 60cm x 60cm (48in x 24in x 24in) or for a dwarf breed 65cm x 65cm x 50cm (26in x 26in x 20in) will be sufficiently large so that it could be used for a doe and litter. Hutches are usually made of wood. Ready-made hutches can be bought at most pet shops, but it will probably be cheaper to make your own. If outdoors, the hutch should be in a sheltered site facing south or south-east in order to catch the sunlight.

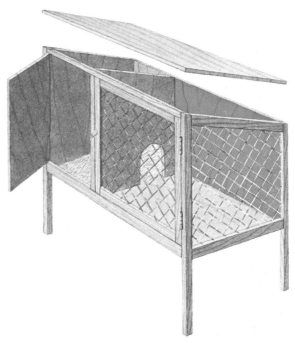

A rabbit hutch should have a sheltered compartment for the rabbit to take refuge in, and should be easy to clean.

General care

When bedding up the rabbit's hutch, place 4-5 layers of newspaper on the floor of the hutch and cover them with a mixture of sawdust and wood shavings to a depth of 5cm (2in). Clean, dry straw or preferably hay can be provided for bedding in the sleeping quarters, and put in the living quarters a stout, bark-covered branch for the rabbit to gnaw on.

Pelleted food or cereal mixes should be provided in a bowl, and a heavy earthenware dog's water bowl is the most suitable. Water may also be provided in these bowls, but it tends to become contaminated with bedding and faeces. Instead, animal drinking bottles fixed outside the cage are the most suitable, especially plastic bottles with a stainless steel sleeve on the end of the drinking tube. There is a tendency for these drinkers to drip excessively, but this can be prevented if two, rather than one, stainless steel balls are present in the sleeve.

The rabbit's feeding bowl and drinking bottle should be cleaned regularly at least weekly.

Cleaning out The hutch must be cleaned out every other day with the bedding in the sleeping quarters changed weekly. Use a short handled shovel or an onion hoe to remove the sawdust directly into a large bucket or bin. At least weekly during the summer, and less frequently during the winter, the hutch should be scrubbed out with a mild disinfectant solution to control the population of flies. Ensure that the hutch has dried out before the rabbit is returned to it. Replace the newspaper and sawdust and return clean portions of the old bedding with some fresh hay into the sleeping quarters. (The old bedding is used to ensure the rabbit returns to a familiar smell.) Store food in sealable plastic containers and buy only sufficient food to last one week, to prevent it becoming stale before use.

Exercise A rabbit needs plenty of exercise and if all escape routes are blocked and you do not mind your prize plants being eaten, it could have access to the garden. If this is unrealistic, a pen can be constructed. The problem is to make it escape-proof despite the burrowing habits of the rabbit. Using existing walls will make construction easier, and wire netting with 2-2½cm (¾-1in) mesh will do for the main portion of the fence. The netting will have to be buried in the ground to a minimum of 30-45cm (12-18in) to thwart tunnelling, with the fence above ground standing at least 1 metre (40in) high.

If an area of lawn is available, all this work can be avoided by the use of a Morant hutch. A rectangular or triangular wooden frame is covered and floored with wire netting, with one end boxed in and floored with wood. A convenient size for such a hutch is 2 metres x 1 metre x 1 metre (80in x 40in x 40in). The wire floor

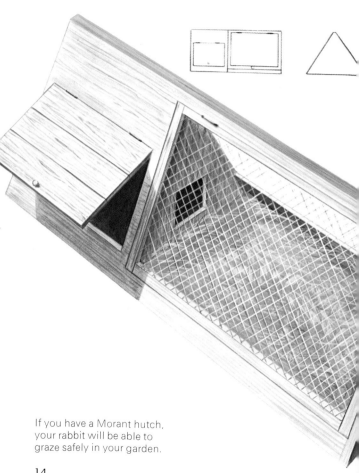

If you have a Morant hutch,
your rabbit will be able to
graze safely in your garden.

14

allows the rabbit to graze without being able to burrow to freedom. This type of hutch must have large doors for easy access to catch the rabbit. The hutch can easily be moved as the grass is eaten, and a rabbit could spend the spring, summer and early autumn in it, but they are unsuitable for winter housing.

Rabbits can be kept in a stack of hutches but make sure there is adequate space and ventilation.

Handling

Always approach the hutch quietly to prevent panic,
talking all the time in a quiet voice. The rabbit will soon
learn to recognize a voice and respond to it. Handle the
rabbit frequently and it will soon become tame.

Rabbits should only be lifted with one hand holding
the scruff of the neck, and with the other hand

Never pick up a rabbit by its
ears. However, you can steady
a rabbit by gently holding the
base of the ears as well as its
rump.

Hold your rabbit by the scruff of the neck and support it with your other hand.

supporting the hind quarters. Rabbits which are incorrectly handled will kick their powerful hind legs or bite. Beware of the rabbit's sharp claws. If whilst handling, a rabbit starts to squeal, gently release it and stroke it until it calms down. This will prevent a sudden death from heart failure. Rabbits can be carried easily if they are allowed to lie along the forearm with the head snuggled into the crook of the arm, which will keep it calm and support its weight.

Grooming

With the exception of the Angora, the grooming of rabbits is not strictly necessary. A healthy rabbit will normally regularly groom itself and provided that the living quarters are adequately maintained, the coat will have a natural bloom.

Regular grooming, however, does give the owner the opportunity to examine the rabbit closely for signs of

The long-haired Angora rabbit needs regular grooming with special brushes and combs.

disease. A table with a non-slip surface, such as sacking or a piece of carpet, will make an ideal grooming table. Grooming brushes and combs specifically designed for small animals can be readily purchased from your pet shop. Daily combing during the rabbit's heavy moult in the autumn will remove large quantities of loose hair.

Parasites Grooming is the ideal time to inspect the coat for parasites. Fleas, ticks, lice and mites can all cause problems in rabbits. Rabbit fleas can be found in the coat during grooming, but are more commonly seen feeding along the edge of the ears. Fleas transmit myxomatosis from wild rabbits to pet rabbits, but can be easily controlled by using flea powder available from pet shops. Ticks sometimes attach themselves to rabbits for up to 3-4 days. During this period, the tick feeds off the rabbit's blood. The tick embeds its mouthparts in the skin and unless it is carefully removed, these will be left behind and will become septic. The tick should be covered with liquid paraffin or vaseline and left for 30 minutes before being gently removed with tweezers. If this procedure worries you, take the rabbit to a vet.

Lice and mites produce similar symptoms of itchiness, hair loss, scurf and scratching. Treatment with flea powder on the rabbit's coat and bedding will normally be successful. Different types of mites can infest the rabbit's ears causing the condition called canker. An infected rabbit shows obvious signs of distress and irritation, scratching at the ears and shaking the head violently. Brown waxy encrustations will become evident in the ear as the condition progresses. If treatment with canker drops from the pet shop does not produce rapid relief, the rabbit should be taken to a vet.

Feeding

Rabbits are herbivores, eating only vegetable matter. They require a varied, balanced diet, fed at regular intervals (two or three times a day). Three different types of food combine to make up a balanced diet.

Dry food Pelleted food or a rabbit mix containing oats, maize and other cereal foods forms the basis of the mixed diet. Feed about a cupful (140-170g/5-6oz) of dry food per day, split into two or three small meals. Toasted stale bread or wheatmeal bread can also be fed.

As well as dry pellets and hay, your pet needs a varied diet of greens and fruit.

Hay Hay should be available throughout the day, but never put more than one day's supply (85g/3oz) in the cage at a time, because it will be trampled on and soiled. Never feed dusty or poor quality hay. If the cage is large enough the hay can be put in a rack on the wall.

Greens A medium-sized rabbit will eat about 450g (16oz) of greens a day. Rabbits fed exclusively on greens will develop digestive problems. A wide variety of wild plants can be collected from the countryside, but not from beside roads because of the lead contamination from car exhaust fumes. Chickweed, comfrey, dandelion, docks, grasses, groundsel, plantain, sow thistles and vetches will all be eaten avidly. If you cannot positively identify a plant, do not feed it to your pet as it may be poisonous.

A variety of vegetables may be fed to rabbits including beans (leaves and pods), broccoli (a good winter feed), cabbage (split the stalks first), spinach and lettuce. Fruit can be fed, but only as titbits, although fruit tree prunings may be given in more substantial amounts. All green foods must be well washed and shaken dry before feeding to prevent leaves soiled by wild rabbits passing any disease to your pet. Root vegetables may be used for winter feed including potato peelings, cooked potato mashed up with an equal amount of bran and raw turnips cut into chips.

Although clover is a very nutritious food, be careful when feeding it to rabbits as excessive amounts can cause a digestive upset called bloat. Definitely poisonous are green raw potatoes, buttercups, foxgloves, geraniums and any evergreen plant.

Water Fresh water must always be available and must be

changed daily. Make certain that does with litters have additional water by filling the container at each feed. In general, pregnant does in the last third of pregnancy and those with young will need two or three times these quantities of food.

Rabbits digest the vegetable matter in an enlarged sac-like organ at the junction of the small and large bowels called the caecum. Nutrients released by the digestion in the caecum can only be absorbed by the rabbit after being re-eaten. Therefore the food passes twice through the digestive tract. The rabbit passes special droppings at

If clean, all of these weeds will be good for your rabbit. (Below) thistle, mare's tail and dock. (Opposite) ribwort plaintain, clover and dandelion.

night which are dark green, soft and shiny and which the rabbit picks from its vent and eats. Rabbits' normal droppings are dry, well formed and hard.

Rabbits with little access to a garden or run for exercise can rapidly become overweight. Large quantities of fat are deposited under the skin and a dewlap may become evident, giving the appearance of a double chin. The only treatment is a combination of exercise and dieting: reduce the amount of food with greenstuffs and bran being increased in the diet and pellets and corn mixtures being decreased.

Breeding and pregnancy

Breeding Eventually many rabbit owners feel they would like to breed at least one litter. Rabbits breed most readily during the spring and early summer; this coincides with the warmer weather which encourages survival and growth of the young and also a plentiful supply of green food.

Sexual maturity in rabbits varies from five months in some dwarf breeds to eight months in the giant breeds. The average pet shop rabbits can usually be bred from six to eight months of age. To prevent any unwanted pregnancies, sexes should be segregated from the age of five months.

The female (doe) is always taken to the male (buck) for

To discover a young rabbit's sex, gently turn it over. The male has a round opening while the female's is V-shaped.

male female

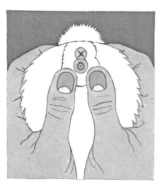
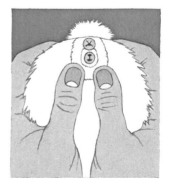

24

A litter of young rabbits inside a nestbox.

mating which occurs very quickly and finishes with the buck falling on his side and making a muted squeal. If mating does not occur soon after the introduction, remove the female to prevent any possible fighting. Re-introduce her daily until mating takes place or try another buck. After mating, return the doe to her hutch.

Pregnancy Pregnancy lasts 30-32 days. During this time the doe should be housed in isolation from other rabbits. She will require little special attention for the first two weeks of pregnancy, but from the 14th day onwards, gradually increase the amount of food so that by the time she gives birth she will be eating twice her normal rations.

During the third week of pregnancy, place a nesting box in the cage plus ample supplies of good quality hay for nesting material. The nest box can be a specially made wooden box measuring 25cm x 30cm x 40cm (10in x 12in x 16in) for the normal pet shop rabbit, or a similarly sized cardboard box. Nest building usually

Two Dutch rabbits with their offspring.

takes place from the 25th day onwards. A few days before giving birth, the doe will pluck fur from her abdomen to line the nest. Handle the doe as little as possible during pregnancy and try to avoid any unnecessary disturbances e.g. barking dogs and marauding cats.

Rabbits will produce litters containing 1-13 babies (kittens). Dwarf breeds tend to have smaller litters, with medium-sized rabbits having an average of six. Do not interfere with the nest after the doe has given birth for at least 4-5 days before enticing the doe off the nest with some food. You can then examine the kittens and remove any dead or deformed ones. Kittens are born naked, blind and deaf and are completely dependent on the mother. By the tenth day their eyes will be open and fur will have grown, but they do not leave the nest for at least 2-3 weeks.

Because of the demands of milk production, the doe will require a continued increase in her food intake, so that by seven days after giving birth she will be eating up to three times her usual amount of food. The doe will suckle the young for about 6-7 weeks, when her milk will start to dry up. Most litters can be weaned from 7-9 weeks. By this time the doe will have lost condition and be very thin, but this is quite normal. Offer the youngsters solid food from 3-4 weeks of age. Although a doe can be mated again soon after weaning, it is advisable to restrict her to no more than three litters per year.

Pseudo pregnancy Not every mating leads to a true pregnancy. Some does will apparently conceive and go through all the actions leading to giving birth 16-18 days after mating, but no young will result.

27

Diseases

It is advisable to isolate a sick rabbit and to seek veterinary advice as soon as possible. Rabbits will soon succumb to many diseases without early treatment and careful nursing. Some diseases can be transmitted to man, particularly children, so follow these rules:

1 Wash your hands after handling the rabbit or cleaning out the hutch.
2 Wash the rabbit's bowls and water bottles separately from the household crockery.
3 Rabbit food must be stored separately from the owner's food in sealable containers to prevent access to vermin.
4 Animals must not be brought into food preparation or storage areas.
5 Never eat or drink whilst playing with a rabbit or when cleaning out the hutch.
6 Young children must be supervised by adults to ensure these rules are adhered to.

Use sharp nail clippers to trim the tips of your rabbit's nails. Make certain you do not cut the vein, which is clearly visible.

Ailments

Overgrown claws Rabbit's claws may need cutting once or twice a year. Once you have seen how to clip the nails it is easy (see illustration).

Heat stroke Most common in pregnant does; remove the hutch from direct sunlight.

Mucoid enteritis Diarrhoea containing mucous. There will be dehydration and death if untreated. Prevent the disease by ensuring adequate hay in the diet.

Myxomatosis Rare in pet rabbits. It causes swelling of the eyelids, nose and anus followed by death and is transmitted by fleas. A vaccine is available.

Overgrown teeth Symptoms are a ragged, unkempt coat, drooling and inability to eat. Prevent it by providing hard food, e.g. sprout stalks and branches with bark.

Paralysis The main cause is mishandling. Always support the hind quarters when lifting a rabbit. Close confinement may aid recovery.

Ringworm A fungal disease causing circular patches on the head and feet. It can be infectious to children handling infected animals.

Snuffles A common infectious disease of young kittens of 3-4 weeks of age. Symptoms include sneezing and a watery nose and eyes. Infected rabbits may rapidly worsen developing a pneumonia, or the disease can become more chronic with the discharges becoming thicker. Early treatment may be successful, but there is no known treatment for chronically infected individuals.

Sore hocks Obesity and dirty housing conditions can cause the development of open sores on the rabbit's hocks. Bathe sores with a salt solution and provide a deep, clean bed.

Exhibiting

Having kept and bred rabbits successfully for a number of years, many owners start to think about showing. This is the time when visiting shows, looking at winning rabbits and talking to exhibitors will pay dividends. It is from contacts made at these shows that you will learn of a source of good quality 'pure' breeding stock to start your strain of show rabbits.

Exhibiting at local shows may be unrestricted (open to everyone), but only registered rabbits may be exhibited in shows run under the auspices of the British Rabbit

Rabbits being exhibited in show pens.

Council (BRC). If you want to exhibit seriously, you must register with the BRC.

Registered rabbits are identified by rings which are supplied by the BRC to individual breeders. These 'show rings' are slipped onto the hind leg of the rabbit, above the hock, when it is 8-12 weeks old. As the rabbit grows, the ring can no longer be slid over the hock and it therefore permanently identifies the rabbit.

Rabbits must be carefully prepared for exhibiting by good feeding, grooming and careful, regular handling. Rabbits younger than four months can be exhibited in special classes, but they are not at their best until aged at least 6-8 months. A travelling box is the only major item of additional equipment – this can be a simple cardboard 'cat box' for the smaller breeds or a more expensive purpose-built wooden box. Cover the floor with sawdust and put in some hay and toast for the rabbit to eat, but do not include any greens as they tend to be trampled on and soiled.

ADDRESSES
The Secretary, British Rabbit Council, Purefoy House, 7 Kirkgate, Newark, Nottinghamshire NG24 1AD.
The Royal Society for the Prevention of Cruelty to Animals, Causeway, Horsham, Sussex RH12 1HG.

Index